NOTES TO PEOPLE
ELIZABETH KUEHNE

IMPORTANT NOTICE

Copyright © Engage Editing Press. All rights reserved.

Engage Editing Press owns or controls all proprietary rights and copyrights to the content contained herein. Except as provided for under a license agreement, no part of this publication may be transferred, resold (in part or whole), file-shared, copied, reproduced, modified, stored in a retrieval system, transmitted (e.g. sent via email), or made public (e.g. posted to Slideshare, Facebook, YouTube) in any form without the express written permission of Engage Editing Press. Engage Editing Press may pursue criminal and civil claims for any unauthorized use, misappropriation, or distribution of any content contained herein.

ABOUT ENGAGE EDITING PRESS

Engage Editing Press is a small business specializing in leadership, education, self-care, and personal growth. We have two writers, one editor, and two dogs who run the show. We require caffeine to function. We expect you might too.

Our purpose is to help individuals achieve growth and results as professionals and as individuals acting in harmony with one another in society. We believe in the inherent goodness of all persons and dogs of the world.

For inquiries, please email the editors at engageeditingpress@gmail.com .

We would love to hear from you.

©2021

TO YOU, DEAR READER:

Every day I have interactions with people that I never actually complete. It might be as quick as a passing glance, or maybe a long observation, but there are usually things I want to say, but don't. Or, there may be things I think about saying later, but have lost the opportunity. The impetus for this text is simply that. I saw a man in a grocery store and he saw me, and we walked past each other with not a word, but only the vaguest of smiles and the quickest of glances. And as I walked on, I thought, "We could have been made for each other." The thing is, those interactions happen constantly and consistently on so many levels. It doesn't have to be an interaction that we think might be fate, but it could be an observation of someone who has not been observed before...or who deserves to be observed.

Let's face it: we live in a culture of mean, and we see it daily in social media. Sure, social media has its fair share of heroes who are also trying to change the culture, but in the end, I see that we are often less genuine, less consistent, and certainly less supportive of one another. So I decided to start writing notes. It became notes to people. And to be clear, most of these are people I will probably never see ever again. Maybe they are people I will never even think about again. And I don't expect to have them seek me out, either. Some of them are people who are in my daily life because I think about them daily, but most of them are people I've had the most superficial and simple of relationships with. We've shared airspace. If that isn't the most intimate of things, I'm not sure what is.

So read them one at a time, or binge on them, or write your own notes to people. I hope you enjoy it. Oh, dear reader, you'll find several notes to you, as well. Maybe you'll even find a thought you've had. Enjoy.

TO THE GIRL IN THE PURPLE SWEATSHIRT,

TO THE GIRL IN THE PURPLE SWEATSHIRT, WHITE SWEATBAND AND PERKY PONYTAIL: THANK YOU FOR INSPIRING ME TO WRITE NOTES TO PEOPLE. I WAS INSPIRED BY YOU BECAUSE IT IS COLD OUT THERE, AND YOU WERE RUNNING EARLY IN THE DAY, FROST BLOOMING FROM YOUR EXHALATIONS, YOUR ARM STRETCHED IN FRONT AS YOUR DOG JOGGED BESIDE YOU. THE LEASH WAS WRAPPED AROUND YOUR WRIST, AND IT APPEARED FINE, UNTIL YOU WERE JERKED TO THE RIGHT WHEN YOUR DOG SMELLED SOMETHING OR SOMEONE. IT MAY HAVE BEEN ANOTHER DOG, OR A GIRL, OR MAYBE A SKUNK. YOU ALMOST LOST YOUR ARM, BUT YOU WENT WITH HIM AND THAT'S BECAUSE YOU LOVE HIM. YOU MAY NOT HAVE HAD A GREAT RUN, BUT YOU TRIED, AND YOU INSPIRED ME. SO, THANKS. I APPRECIATE YOU.

TO THE ANGRY MAN IN THE GROCERY STORE

TO THE ANGRY MAN IN THE GROCERY STORE WHO WAS YELLING AT HIS WIFE: WHAT HAPPENED TODAY? WHY ARE YOU SO ANGRY? IS SHE A BAD WOMAN? DID SHE DROP THE PUMPKIN ON YOUR TOE? DID YOU LOSE YOUR JOB? DID YOUR CAR DIE ON THE FREEWAY, OR YOUR THERMOSTAT GO OUT, OR YOUR WINDSHIELD CRACK? I KNOW HOW FRUSTRATING THAT CAN BE.

ARE YOU HUNGRY? TIRED? UNHAPPY?

I TRY TO UNDERSTAND, BUT I CANNOT. THERE IS NO EXCUSE FOR TREATING HER LIKE LESS THAN YOUR DOG, NO MATTER WHAT HAPPENED TODAY. SHE IS WITH YOU BECAUSE SHE SEES SOMETHING IN YOU THAT I CANNOT. I APPLAUD HER. BUT MAYBE, SHE'S NOT SO GREAT, EITHER. REGARDLESS, DO YOU NEED TO BELITTLE HER, DEMEAN HER, DESTROY HER, IN PUBLIC? IN FRONT OF THOSE WHO I PRESUME ARE YOUR CHILDREN, SINCE THEY BOTH CLUNG TO THE TWO OF YOU. DO YOU SEE HOW ALL THREE ARE IN TEARS?

TO THE GIRL WHO CAN'T COOK YET:

TO THE GIRL WHO CAN'T COOK YET: YOU WILL LEARN. HANG IN THERE. YOU JUST HAVE TO TAKE SOME RISKS SOMETIMES. YOU WILL PROBABLY SCREW UP. MAYBE EVEN A LOT. BUT HEY, START WITH THE THINGS YOU LIKE, AND GET GOOD AT COOKING THOSE THINGS. REMEMBER, MORE SPICE IS NOT BETTER THAN LESS. ESPECIALLY SALT. BUT, YOU'LL GET THE KNACK BEFORE YOU KNOW IT. PAY ATTENTION TO WHAT YOU DO WHEN YOU ARE DOING IT SO THAT YOU KNOW WHEN SOMETHING IS GOOD. WHEN IT'S BAD, PAY ATTENTION TO THAT TOO.

TRUST ME, I'VE HAD SOME DAYS WHEN I DIDN'T THINK I WAS GOING TO GET MY FAMILY FED. BUT THEY SURVIVED. IT HAPPENS. JUST KEEP AT IT. GET TO KNOW SOME FAVORITES, AND ROTATE THEM WITH NEW EXPERIENCES. YOU GOT THIS, SISTER.

TO THE PEOPLE WHO DON'T READ EMAILS THOROUGHLY,

TO THE PEOPLE WHO DON'T READ EMAILS THOROUGHLY. SIGH. WHAT IS WRONG WITH YOU?

READ IT. READ IT AGAIN. THEN WAIT TO RESPOND. EVEN 10 SECONDS. CONSIDER IT, THINK IT THROUGH, THEN CHECK IT AGAIN. I BET THE INFORMATION YOU WANT IS THERE IF YOU LOOK AGAIN. AND MAYBE IT ISN'T. SO MAKE SURE YOU PLAN YOUR QUESTIONS PROPERLY SO YOU GET WHAT YOU WANT TO KNOW FROM THE PEOPLE WHO HAVE THE INFO.

DEAR NEIGHBOR WHO JUST MOVED IN:

DEAR NEIGHBOR WHO JUST MOVED IN: I HATE YOUR DOG. HE BARKS AT ME WHEN I AM IN MY OWN YARD, AND HE COMES OVER AND POOPS NEXT TO MY TRASH CAN. I'M AFRAID TO WALK OUT IN THE DARK IN MY SLIPPERS, BECAUSE I MIGHT TRACK THAT SHIT IN. I BET HE IS A GREAT DOG, AND HE PROBABLY COMES TO YOU WHEN YOU CALL TO HIM, BUT HE IS TERRORIZING MY DOGS, KEEPING ME AWAKE AT NIGHT, AND THE OTHER DAY HE JUMPED UP ON THE HOOD OF MY CAR AND SCRABBLED AT WHATEVER CREATURE MUST HAVE HIDDEN UNDER IT. MY PAINT IS RUINED.

TO THE MAN WHO GESTICULATED MADLY

To the man who gesticulated madly as he honked on his horn and counted off cars behind the little old lady with the silvery curls...she was simply being cautious. Come on, man, she was in a 1998 Toyota Tercel and could barely see over the wheel, and you were in such a hurry that you made yourself look really, rather silly. I mean, I thought you looked silly. It made me think of the time I did that to someone and my son looked me square in the face and told me I looked silly. That's rough. When your kid looks you in the face and tells you that you look stupid? Well, you didn't have anyone to tell you that, but you have me, now. I wish you had been a bit more patient, but you weren't. You honked again, and the guy behind you honked at you, because when it was his turn at the light, I could see he was definitely finding humor in the situation. I mean, he had a passenger, so maybe she had just told him a joke or something, but I think you might have been the joke, buddy.

TO THE 73 YEAR OLD WOMAN WITH THE SILVERY HAIR

TO THE 73 YEAR OLD WOMAN WITH THE SILVERY HAIR AND THE HIGH BOOTS WHO DRIVES TO THE RURAL RESERVATIONS TO WORK WITH INDIGENTS...YOU ARE AMAZING. I KNOW YOU WEAR THE BOOTS BECAUSE THE DOGS IN THOSE AREAS ARE UNPREDICTABLE AND SOMETIMES SNAP AT YOUR HEELS, AND MORE OFTEN THAN NOT, IT IS MUDDY AND THE GROUNDS ARE HIGH WITH WEEDS. YOU'RE SMART TO DRESS THE WAY YOU DO. I WONDER WHEN YOU WILL RETIRE? I HOPE YOU FIND THE TIME AND MONEY TO BE ABLE TO DO SO. YOU DESERVE IT.

DEAR AIDAN:

Dear Aidan: 18 years ago, at around 3:50 in the afternoon, they dumped you on my stomach. You were gray and bloody and well...kind of ugly. But you took a breath, blinked your eyes, and I realized you were Aidan and I have never been more in love in all my life. That night, your dad and I put you between us on the bed and just gazed at you, and we both teared up, recognizing the enormity of what we had done. I'll never forget that. I hope one day you have a similar experience.

TO FRIENDS WHO ANSWER TEXTS

NOTE TO FRIENDS WHO ANSWER TEXTS IN THE MIDDLE OF THE NIGHT. THANK YOU.

TO THE LONELY MEN WHO ARE SEEKING WOMEN...

TO THE LONELY MEN WHO ARE SEEKING WOMEN...FOR A LITTLE WHILE: DON'T BOTHER. YOU ARE BEING SELFISH. IF YOU ARE MARRIED, EMOTIONALLY UNAVAILABLE, IN IT SIMPLY FOR SEX, OR SIMPLY BECAUSE YOU NEED A DISTRACTION, THEN DON'T ENGAGE A WOMAN'S HEART NEEDLESSLY. KNOW THYSELF, MAN. I BELIEVE SHAKESPEARE SAID THAT FIRST. NO, MAYBE JESUS DID. AT ANY RATE, KNOW WHAT YOU WANT, AND KNOW WHAT YOU NEED, AND DON'T ALLOW IT TO MOVE TO THE NEXT LEVEL UNLESS YOU ARE CERTAIN YOU WANT TO BE WITH THAT WOMAN, BECAUSE USING HER FOR THE TIME IS HURTFUL.

OF COURSE, THAT IS TRUE OF YOU LADIES. I MEAN IT WOULD BE HYPOCRITICAL TO NOT ADDRESS THE WOMEN WHO ALSO DO THE SAME, BUT IT BOILS DOWN TO HONESTY, LOYALTY AND SELF-UNDERSTANDING. DON'T PLAY GAMES ANYMORE. WE WOULD LIKE TO BELIEVE WE ARE ADULTS AND THAT ADULTS DON'T USE ONE ANOTHER, BUT THEN AGAIN, WHAT DO WE KNOW? THE GUIDEBOOKS ARE FLAWED.

TRUST ME. A WOMAN KNOWS WHEN SHE IS BEING REJECTED.

OKAY, SO BY NOW YOU'RE ROLLING YOUR EYES AND YOU THINK I'M A MAN-HATER. WELL MAYBE SOMETIMES. I HAVE BEEN HURT MANY TIMES BY MANY MEN, AND I KNOW MY COMPLICITY. I HAVE CHOSEN MEN IN MOMENTS OF EMPTINESS MYSELF. PERHAPS I AM AS AT FAULT FOR THE DEVASTATION I EXPERIENCE ON OCCASION. BUT, STILL. IF LONELY, KNOW THYSELF AND KNOW WHY YOU SEEK COMPANY. I WILL WORK AT IT TOO. HONESTY IS TRULY A BEAUTIFUL POLICY.

DEAR OLD LADY:

DEAR OLD LADY: I WISH I WASN'T JUDGING, BUT I AM. THERE YOU ARE, IN YOUR TURQUOISE PANTS AND RED CHENILLE SWEATER WITH THE FUR LINED MOCCASINS, SENDING MONEY TO YOUR DAUGHTER. I OVERHEARD YOUR BIRTHDATE, AND I KNOW YOU ARE ALMOST 87.

I BET YOU WERE A TEACHER, PRIMARILY BECAUSE I SAW YOUR DEBIT CARD AND KNOW IT IS FROM THE EDUCATOR'S CREDIT UNION, BUT BEFORE YOU THINK I'M THAT MUCH OF A STALKER, LET ME ALSO SAY THAT THERE IS AN AIR ABOUT YOU. A PRACTICALITY, EVEN, IN THE WAY YOU DRESS AND THE WAY YOU MOVE. YOU ARE USED TO TAKING CARE OF PEOPLE, AND YOUR DAUGHTER IS YOUR FAVORITE.

SO REALLY, LET'S GET BACK TO THE JUDGING FOR A MOMENT. I THINK YOU ARE BEAUTIFUL. I'M PISSED AT YOUR DAUGHTER, THOUGH. SHE IS SUPPOSED TO BE TAKING CARE OF YOU, AND YET HERE YOU ARE, LEANING ON YOUR SHOPPING CART AND SENDING HER SOME CASH. BUT BEFORE I BECOME TOO FAR OUT OF LINE, LET ME IMAGINE THAT MAYBE YOU ARE SENDING MONEY TO YOUR GRANDDAUGHTER FOR HER BIRTHDAY. OR MAYBE YOU BOUGHT YOUR DAUGHTER A SET OF FURNITURE FOR HER BIRTHDAY, AND SHE PICKED IT OUT IN HER TOWN. MAYBE YOU JUST WANT TO SEND MONEY SO IT ISN'T TIED UP IN PROBATE OR INHERITANCE TAXES WHEN YOU DIE. BUT MAYBE, YOUR DAUGHTER IS TAKING ADVANTAGE OF YOU, AND THAT IS WHAT BOTHERS ME.

DEAR BAR TENDRESS IN THE BLACK HEELS

DEAR BAR TENDRESS IN THE BLACK HEELS AND PRETTY BLACK TOP: WE CAME HERE BECAUSE WE WERE AT THE STORE NEXT DOOR AND WANTED A BEER AND SOME CONVERSATION. IT IS NOT THE NICEST NEIGHBORHOOD, BUT MY FRIEND AND I WERE TIRED BUT NOT QUITE READY TO GO HOME.

IN FACT, THIS PLACE IS KIND OF A DIVE BAR. IT IS WHERE WOMEN OUR AGE GO TO PICK UP MEN OF OUR AGE, BUT THEY ARE NEVER THE MEN WE WANT ONCE WE GET THEM.

BUT YOU ARE ROCKING IT, SISTER. I BET YOU MAKE A LOT OF MONEY WITH ALL OF THE MIDDLE AGED MEN WHO SIT AT YOUR BAR DRINKING DRAFT BEER WHILE THEY WATCH FOOTBALL. I ADMIRE YOU BECAUSE YOU ARE DRESSED TO A TEE, YOUR MAKEUP IS ON POINT, YOUR HAIR IS THICK AND HEALTHY AND RICH, AND YOU HAVE A GOOD SENSE OF YOUR CLIENTELE. IT IS OBVIOUS YOU KNOW WHO YOU ARE.

TO THE MAN IN THE WALKER AT THE GYM

TO THE MAN IN THE WALKER AT THE GYM, MOVING SLOWLY BUT PURPOSEFULLY TO EACH MACHINE ON THE CIRCUIT, YOU INSPIRE ME. YOU TOLD ME YOU WERE PERFECTLY HEALTHY UNTIL THE CAR ACCIDENT, AND I KNOW HOW THAT MUST HAVE CHANGED YOUR WORLD. THANK YOU FOR CONTINUING TO LOVE YOURSELF. THANK YOU FOR NOT GIVING UP.

TO THE GIRL WHO PLAYS

TO THE GIRL WHO PLAYS WORDS WITH FRIENDS LIKE YOU HAVE A KNIFE TO SOMEONE'S THROAT   WOW. WHERE ON EARTH DID YOU COME UP WITH THAT WORD TO GET 127 POINTS? I MEAN, I HAVE A PRETTY WELL ESTABLISHED VOCABULARY, AND I'VE NEVER SEEN THAT LETTER COMBINATION, AND THEN, TO GET TWO TRIPLE LETTER AND TWO TRIPLE WORD SCORES AND USE ALL 7 LETTERS? HOLY MOLEY. YOU'RE GOOD. OR RUTHLESS. OR HEARTLESS. I CANNOT COMPETE. I RESIGN.

TO THE BOY WHO RIDES HIS BIKE

TO THE BOY WHO RIDES HIS BIKE IN THE MIDDLE OF THE ROAD AND FLIPS ME OFF WHEN I GO TO PASS YOU, WHERE ARE YOUR PARENTS? WHY DIDN'T THEY TEACH YOU THAT YOU ARE ACTUALLY THE VULNERABLE ONE HERE? DO YOU NOT REALIZE THAT YOU MUST HAVE TRUST IN ME AND MY SEVERAL THOUSAND POUND CAR, TO KEEP YOU SAFE, AND THAT YOUR LITTLE FINGER THROWING ME THE BIRD DOES TEMPT ME TO VIOLATE GOD'S GREATEST RULE? YOU ARE SO LUCKY MY MOM AND DAD RAISED ME RIGHT, AND THAT I WILL PROTECT YOUR LIFE, EVEN IF I DON'T KNOW YOU, AND EVEN IF I DON'T LIKE YOU.

TO THE BARISTA WHO KNOWS

TO THE BARISTA WHO KNOWS HOW I LIKE MY COFFEE, EVEN THOUGH I AM ONLY IN HERE ONCE A MONTH OR SO   I LOVE YOU. THANK YOU FOR KNOWING MY COFFEE. I WANT TO TIP YOU TEN DOLLARS ON A TWO DOLLAR COFFEE, BUT THEN I CANNOT BUY LUNCH TODAY. I WILL SMILE AT YOU INSTEAD, AND TIP YOU TWO DOLLARS ON MY TWO DOLLAR COFFEE AND YOU WILL BE GRACIOUS BECAUSE EVEN IF I ONLY TIPPED YOU THE CHANGE FROM THE THREE DOLLARS I USE TO PAY FOR THE CUP OF JOE, YOU ARE A KIND AND GENEROUS PERSON WITH A GOOD HEART. I APPRECIATE YOU.

TO THE OTHER BARISTA

TO THE OTHER BARISTA WHO REQUIRES THAT I EXPLAIN MYSELF, AND THEN, INSTEAD OF RINGING IT IN AND THEN GOING TO GET IT STARTED WHILE I GET MY MONEY OUT, YOU SIT AND MAKE SURE TO TAKE MY MONEY FIRST, EVEN THOUGH I'M IN HERE TWO OR THREE TIMES A WEEK. I HAVE WORKED IN FOOD FOR MANY YEARS OF MY LIFE AND KNOW THAT PRIORITIZATION IS AN EXTRAORDINARY SKILL. YOU KNOW THAT IT IS EARLY MORNING, AND THAT I HAVE TO GET TO WORK. YOU'VE SEEN ME IN HERE ENOUGH TO KNOW THAT USUALLY I'M CHOMPING AT THE BIT, ONE BECAUSE I NEED COFFEE, AND TWO, BECAUSE I HAVE TO HIT THE ROAD. I KNOW THAT ISN'T YOUR FAULT, BUT I ALSO KNOW THAT YOU CAN GO OFF AND MAKE THE COFFEE AND THEN MAKE THE CHANGE. ESPECIALLY BECAUSE YOU KNOW AS WELL AS I DO THAT I AM GOING TO TIP YOU REGARDLESS. MAKE IT A SMOOTHER AM, WOULDJA?

DEAR PERSON WHO JUST NEEDS TO SPEAK:

DEAR PERSON WHO JUST NEEDS TO SPEAK: WHEN YOU SUCK IN A BREATH AND THEN SPEND 24 SECONDS APOLOGIZING FOR INTERRUPTING AND THAT YOU DON'T WANT TO INTERRUPT, BUT THEN YOU INTERRUPT ANYWAY AND KEEP TALKING   EITHER SHUT THE F UP, OR SPIT IT OUT, JUNIOR. AND YOU MIGHT WANT TO JUST KEEP THAT BREATH IN YOUR THROAT AND NOT EXPEL THAT BULLSHIT. DON'T POLLUTE THE ROOM WITH YOUR GARBAGE. SOMETIMES YOU COME UP WITH BRILLIANCE, BUT IT DOESN'T ALWAYS HAPPEN, SO I WANT TO SEE THAT YOU ARE REALLY FOCUSED AND GET YOUR SHIT DOWN.

TO THE PERSON WHO MAKES SCALES:

TO THE PERSON WHO MAKES SCALES: CAN YOU CONSIDER SOME ALTERNATIVES? LIKE CREATING A SCALE THAT I CAN REMOVE 10 POUNDS FROM IN ORDER TO TRICK MYSELF? I MEAN, THAT WOULD BE GREAT. IF I POOP, I CAN PROBABLY REDUCE A POUND OR TWO. ON SOME DAYS, MAYBE AS MANY AS FIVE. BUT TODAY, I SEEM TO HOLD STEADY AT A WEIGHT I'M NOT THRILLED ABOUT. SO WHAT DO YOU SAY? HOW ABOUT A SCALABLE SCALE? THAT SOUNDS LIKE A FANTASTIC IDEA TO ME. IN FACT, I'M KIND OF EXCITED ABOUT THAT IDEA. I'D PAY GOOD MONEY FOR THAT.

TO THE TALL DRINK OF WATER

TO THE TALL DRINK OF WATER WALKING DOWN CENTRAL IN A MUSTARD YELLOW LEATHER JACKET AND A DARK FEDORA, WITH YOUR TAILORED PANTS AND OSTRICH LEATHER SHOES, I ADMIRE YOU. I DON'T KNOW WHERE YOU ARE GOING, OR WHAT YOU ARE DOING, BUT SOMEHOW, IT DOESN'T SEEM TO MATTER   EITHER TO ME, OR TO YOU. YOU ARE CHILLIN'. AND YOU LOOK FANTASTIC DOING IT. OKAY, I DON'T KNOW IF THOSE SHOES ARE OSTRICH, BUT SOMEHOW, THAT MAKES NO DIFFERENCE. THE IMAGE FITS. YOU ARE ROCKING IT, AND I LIKE WATCHING YOU.

TO THE PEOPLE WHO CHANGE MY NAME

TO THE PEOPLE WHO CHANGE MY NAME TO SOMETHING THEY PREFER TO CALL ME, OTHER THAN WHAT I WANT TO BE CALLED, OR LIKE TO BE CALLED: STOP. YOU DON'T HAVE TO CONTROL THIS PARTICULAR SITUATION. I INTRODUCED MYSELF IN A SPECIFIC WAY, AND YOU DON'T HAVE PERMISSION TO SHORTEN MY NAME WITHIN FIVE MINUTES OF KNOWING ME. I MAY HAVE BEEN KNOWN BY A SHORTENED VERSION OF MY NAME AT ONE POINT IN MY LIFE, BUT NOW I HAVE MADE AN ADULT CHOICE TO HONOR THE NAME THAT WAS CHOSEN FOR ME, THAT HONORS MY LINEAGE AND MY PATRONAGE, AND THAT SUITS ME AND MY PERSONALITY. AND, BY THE WAY, THAT NAME IS REALLY RATHER BEAUTIFUL.

TO THE LADY WHO HAS TOO MANY HORSES AND DOGS AND CATS

TO THE LADY WHO HAS TOO MANY HORSES AND DOGS AND CATS, BUT NEVER TURNS AN ANIMAL IN NEED AWAY, I WISH YOU HAD A BIGGER HOUSE AND MORE MONEY. I WISH YOU HAD PEOPLE WHO HAULED HAY FOR YOU AND WHO WOULD COLLECT YOUR CHICKEN EGGS WHILE YOU WERE GONE FOR THE WEEKEND. I KNOW YOU WON'T GO FOR THE WEEKEND THOUGH, BECAUSE YOU HAVE TOO MUCH NEED TO TAKE CARE OF THOSE ANIMALS. I WOULD TAKE YOU TO LUNCH THOUGH, MOM. YOU INSPIRE ME TOO.

TO THE MAN WHO SHUT THE DOOR ON MY FINGER

TO THE MAN WHO SHUT THE DOOR ON MY FINGER..I STILL HAVE A SCAR ON MY RING FINGER FROM THE SUNNY AFTERNOON IN SANTA BARBARA WHEN YOU RACED PAST ME TO GET IN THE BATHROOM FIRST. IT MUST HAVE BEEN AN EMERGENCY. I HOPE IT ALL TURNED OUT OKAY.

TO THE MAN WHO LOST A SINGLE SHOE

TO THE MAN WHO LOST A SINGLE SHOE ON THE SIDE OF THE FREEWAY...JUST ONE QUESTION   HOW? OKAY, I CAN'T STOP THERE. WERE YOU HANGING YOUR FEET OUT THE WINDOW AND A WIND GUST TOOK IT? DID YOU KICK THE MIRROR AND IT SLIPPED OFF? DID YOU THROW IT AT A FLY AND FORGET THE WINDOW WAS OPEN? I'M JUST SO CURIOUS. I'VE NEVER LOST A SHOE ON THE FREEWAY.

TO THE LADY MELTING DOWN

TO THE LADY MELTING DOWN BEHIND ME IN THE SHERATON LOBBY BAR YOU ARE SCARING ME. WHAT'S HAPPENING HERE? THERE SEEMS TO BE A CONFLICT BETWEEN YOU AND THE BAR STAFF, BUT THEY ARE IGNORING YOU. YOU ARE POUNDING YOUR HANDS AGAINST THE CHAIR IN OBVIOUS DISTRESS AND RAGE. I WANT TO PAY YOUR BILL, BUT I KNOW THEY CAN COMP YOUR TICKET IF NECESSARY. I HATE YOUR STRESS.

TO THE SAME LADY

To the same lady who, ten minutes later, is still fuming...baby girl...walk away. Find your center. Let it ride. People are starting to talk about you. It's starting to be a public scene. Don't let that happen. Find grace in what you do next. Be graceful.

TO EARL,

TO EARL, WHO IS CURRENTLY SINGING PENNIES FROM HEAVEN TO PENNY, ANOTHER GUEST. KEEP SINGING, SOLDIER.

HE SAYS HE SINGS ON THE INTERCOM ON SOUTHWEST WHEN HE FLIES BECAUSE HE WANTS TO MAKE EVERYONE HAPPY. HE IS A RETIRED NAVY PILOT WHO FLEW IN WWII.

EARL: YOU'VE EARNED YOUR SONGS. WE ALL HAVE ENJOYED YOU.

TO THE WOMAN FRANTICALLY CALLING FOR RILEY

TO THE WOMAN FRANTICALLY CALLING FOR RILEY IN THE BALTIMORE AIRPORT LADIES ROOM, I'M GOING TO SAY THAT BY YOUR 6TH OR 8TH PASS, AND EACH MORE PANICKED THAN THE LAST, THROUGH THAT ROOM...AND WITH YOUR BOOMING VOICE...IT'S PROBABLY TIME TO GET AIRPORT SECURITY TO HELP YOU FIND YOUR GIRL. THAT, OR HER HEADPHONES ARE GOING INTO THE VERY THRONE UPON WHICH SHE SITS. YOU EITHER NEED BETTER GROUND RULES, OR RILEY NEEDS A SPANKING. AIRPORTS AND MISSING KIDS ARE NOT NEARLY AS FUN AS THE MOVIES WILL MAKE THEM OUT TO BE.

TO THE FAKE LAUGHER

TO THE FAKE LAUGHER AT THE TABLE NEXT TO ME...THE SMILE DOESN'T EVEN HIT YOUR EYES. WHY MAKE THAT INGRATIATING NOISE JUST TO PLEASE SOMEONE? IF YOU MUST FAKE A LAUGH, WHAT ELSE IS FAKE IN YOUR LIFE? HOW MANY GOOD THINGS HAVE YOU MISSED BECAUSE YOU WANT SOMETHING MORE THAN WHAT YOU ARE GETTING? HOW MANY TIMES HAVE YOU FELT DISAPPOINTMENT AND COVERED IT WITH A SIGH OR AN EXCUSE? I FEEL YOUR LONELINESS. I HOPE YOU EXPERIENCE LIFE DIFFERENTLY THAN I OBSERVE.

TO THE LOUDMOUTH

TO THE LOUDMOUTH AT THE TABLE FULL OF WOMEN: YOU ARE NOT CHARMING. YOU ARE OBNOXIOUS AND THE LADIES ARE OBVIOUSLY MERELY TOLERATING YOU BECAUSE YOU ALLOW THEM A MOMENT TO SIT BACK AND NOT HAVE TO BE "ON." OR MAYBE YOU ARE THE BOSS. IT IS OBVIOUS THAT YOU ARE A SALESMAN, AND YOU ARE THE PUSHY TYPE, AT THAT. FOR ONCE, SIT BACK AND LISTEN TO WHAT SOMEONE ELSE HAS TO SAY.

TO THE WAITRESS

TO THE WAITRESS WHO IS TRYING SO HARD TO KEEP OUT OF THE WEEDS--YOU ARE DOING A GOOD JOB. YOU FORGOT MY KETCHUP AND MY WATER NEEDS REFILLING, BUT YOU'VE GIVEN ME PLENTY OF TIME TO OBSERVE PEOPLE IN THE TIME YOU'VE BEEN DISTRACTED BY OTHER TABLES. I WILL SURVIVE. I MEAN, IT IS GETTING HOT OUT HERE, AND I AM A BIT PARCHED, BUT I HAVE ICE STILL MELTING IN MY GLASS, AND THAT MEANS I WON'T DIE. YOU DID BRING MY FOOD WHILE IT WAS HOT, AND I HAVE MY LINEN AND SILVERWARE. YOU SMILED AT ME WHEN YOU TOOK CARE OF ME AND YOU TOOK ONE EXTRA SECOND TO MAKE SURE I HAD THE FOOD I WANTED THE WAY I WANTED IT. LIFE IS GOOD. THANK YOU.

TO THE FURNITURE SALESMAN

   TO THE FURNITURE SALESMAN WHO TRIED TO CONVINCE ME THAT NO LEATHER FURNITURE IS TRULY LEATHER, BUT INSTEAD, IT IS ALWAYS SOME SORT OF SYNTHETIC   THAT IS SOME NEXT LEVEL BULLSHIT.

WHAT DO YOU THINK HUGH HEFNER WOULD SAY TO YOUR SALES PITCH? I'M PRETTY SURE HE'D LOOK YOU AS DIRECTLY IN THE EYE AS YOU ARE LOOKING AT ME AND TELL YOU THAT YOU ARE FULL OF SHIT. LEATHER FURNITURE HAS BEEN AROUND PROBABLY ALMOST AS LONG AS HUMANS AND COWS HAVE BEEN IN CLOSE PROXIMITY. I MEAN, I MIGHT BE LOADING MY OWN PILE THERE, BUT IT MAKES SENSE. COWHIDE IS ONE OF THE TOUGHEST MATERIALS...AND LIGHTEST...THAT EXISTS FOR TURNING ONE THING INTO ANOTHER.

TO THE OLDER WOMAN

TO THE OLDER WOMAN WITH THE DARKLY TANNED SKIN, THE MOUTHFUL OF EXPENSIVE TEETH, THE DARK HAIR DYE JOB AND THE CUTEST LITTLE SWIM COVER I'VE EVER SEEN, I'M SORRY TO OVERHEAR YOUR CONVERSATION WITH YOUR FRIEND. THE FACT THAT YOU JUST TOLD HER THAT YOU "FINALLY FEEL CUTE" SADDENS ME. I THINK YOU'RE A BIT OVERDONE, BUT CUTE AS A BUTTON, AND IT DOESN'T MATTER WHAT I THINK ANYWAY. YOU HAVE LIVED TOO MANY YEARS TO DEFINE YOURSELF BY OTHERS. YOU HAVE EARNED EVERY DAY OF CUTENESS. YOU ARE CUTE. YOU PROBABLY ARE WONDERFUL. CUT YOURSELF SOME SLACK. I'M JUST GLAD YOU HAVE A FRIEND THAT YOU CAN CONFIDE THAT LITTLE NUGGET TO. I'M SORRY I JUST SOLD YOU OUT. IF YOU ARE READING THIS, YOU'RE CUTE EVERY DAY, LADY.

TO THE PEOPLE WHO GET TO

TO THE PEOPLE WHO GET TO WEAR UNIFORMS TO WORK EVERY DAY: YOU ARE SO LUCKY. I KNOW THERE ARE MANY OF YOU WHO ARE BORED TO DEATH WITH THE UNIFORM YOU WEAR, BUT GOSH, TO NOT HAVE TO MAKE A SINGLE CHOICE ABOUT THE COLOR, OR THE PATTERN, OR THE MATCHING OF THE BLOUSE WITH THE SLACKS...AND THE MONEY YOU MUST SAVE! MY CLOSET IS PACKED WITH CRAP I AM TOO COLD TO WEAR, OR THAT ISN'T "WORK APPROPRIATE" OR HOWEVER THAT WORKS. I THINK WE LONG FOR THE THINGS WE CANNOT HAVE. I LONG TO WEAR A UNIFORM.

TO THE SPEAKERS OF SINGSONG

TO THE SPEAKERS OF SINGSONG...OY VEY. I GET IT THAT WE SHOULD MODERATE OUR VOICE FOR INTEREST AND INFORMATION ATTAINMENT, BUT OFFICE SPACE HAD IT SO RIGHT WHEN THEY NAILED THAT ONE SECRETARY WHO SPOKE IN HER CONSISTENT RHYTHM. IT'S ANNOYING AS ALL GET OUT TO HEAR A COMMENTARY IN SINGSONG. THAT'S WHY WE STOPPED DOING THAT AFTER 2ND GRADE.

ALSO. TO THE SPEAKERS WHO

ALSO. TO THE SPEAKERS WHO END THEIR AFFIRMATIVE STATEMENTS IN QUESTIONS...DO YOU THINK YOU NEED AN ANSWER TO A STATEMENT? OR IS IT SIMPLY AN AFFECT THAT YOU'VE SOMEHOW COME BY? DID YOU SKIP THAT LESSON IN 2ND GRADE ALSO? QUESTIONS END IN A RAISED VOICE, STATEMENTS END IN A RESOUNDING CONCLUSION. PERIOD, EXCLAMATION POINT, OR, AS I MIGHT ARGUE HERE, THE EVER LOVING ELLIPSIS THAT DRAGS OUT A THOUGHT OR TWO. I LOVE THEM.

TO THE OLD COUPLES

TO THE OLD COUPLES MARRIED 50 YEARS, OR 60 YEARS, OR 63 YEARS...HOW DID YOU DO IT? HOW DID YOU SURVIVE THE LONG NIGHTS AND THE COLD DAYS? MAYBE THE DAYS ARE LONG, BUT THE YEARS ARE SHORT, AND MAYBE, YOU CHOSE THE BEST PARTNER YOU EVER COULD IMAGINE.

TO THE WOMAN WHO CANNOT

TO THE WOMAN WHO CANNOT MAKE A DECISION FOR HERSELF AND LOOKS TO HER HUSBAND EVEN FOR WHAT WINE SHE WANTS TO DRINK FOR PLEASURE...SIGH. I COULD NEVER BE YOU. I THINK YOUR SYSTEM MUST WORK FOR YOU, BUT IT DEPRESSES ME. I KNOW WHAT I LIKE, AND I USUALLY KNOW WHAT I WANT. AND ONCE I'VE DECIDED I KNOW WHAT I LIKE, AND THEN, WHAT I WANT, I GO GET IT. LIKE THE WATCH ON MY WRIST, OR THE WINE IN MY GLASS, OR THE STEAK I'M EATING. I WONDER WHAT YOUR DAILY LIFE LOOKS LIKE. DO YOU HAVE TO ASK HIM WHAT HE WANTS FOR DINNER--AND THEN DOES HE ANSWER? I REMEMBER ASKING MY SON EVERY DAY OF HIS TEENAGED YEARS WHAT HE WANTED FOR DINNER, AND IT ALWAYS CAME BACK TO ME TRYING TO USE MY WORN OUT IMAGINATION TO FEED HIM SOMETHING HE'D ENJOY THAT WOULD ALSO BE SEMI-NUTRITIOUS AND REQUIRE MINIMAL COOK TIME, AND MINIMAL DISHWASHING. MAYBE THAT IS PARTLY WHERE OUR DIFFERENCE LIES. I HOPE YOUR PARTNER CHOOSES A GOOD WINE FOR YOU.

TO THE BALLHOUND

TO THE BALLHOUND WHO GAVE ME HIS 1,448TH HOME RUN BALL FROM THE CLEVELAND INDIANS WHEN THEY PLAYED AT CAMDEN YARDS ONE SUMMER, THANK YOU. I KNOW MY SON AND I WERE A SIGHT, SITTING IN THE BLEACHERS IN OUR ORANGE PLASTIC PONCHOS BECAUSE A STORM WAS THREATENING AND EVERY SINGLE OTHER FAN HAD ALREADY RUN FOR THE HILLS TO GET SHELTER THANK YOU. WE FLEW ACROSS THE COUNTRY FOR THAT GAME, AND WE WEREN'T GOING TO MISS A SECOND OF IT. WHILE MY SON WAS READY FOR A NAP AND WAS NOT NEARLY AS INTERESTED IN WHAT WAS ABOUT TO HAPPEN AS I WAS, YOU MADE THE EVENT SOMETHING TO REMEMBER. NOW, I'M NOT KNOCKING IT, BUT HAVING MANNY MACHADO'S HOMERUN BALL MIGHT HAVE BEEN SOMETHING I VALUED A BIT MORE BUT NONETHELESS, YOU FOUND US IRRESISTIBLE AND YOU THOUGHT WE DESERVED AN AWARD FOR BEING "TRUE FANS." THANKS. THOSE ARE THE MEMORIES I TREASURE.

TO THE GIRL WHO USES 37 WORDS

TO THE GIRL WHO USES 37 WORDS WHEN 2 WOULD SUFFICE — WHY? YOU ARE THE GIRL WHO SKEWS THE AVERAGE FOR WOMEN'S VOCABULARY USAGE. I GET IT THAT MEN AND WOMEN COMMUNICATE DIFFERENTLY, AND I AM NOT MAKING THIS A SEXIST THING. I MEAN, I'M A WOMAN TOO. BUT WHY NOT JUST SAY, FOR EXAMPLE, "NO" AND LEAVE IT AT THAT? WHY AN EXPLANATION THAT VERGES ON HYSTERIA? I STOPPED LISTENING FAR TOO LONG AGO, AND I'M OF THE FAIRER SEX TOO. I'M SYMPATHETIC TO YOU, BUT YOU EXHAUST ME. JUST, PLEASE, STOP TALKING.

DEAR WOMEN WHOM I HAVE JUST OFFENDED

DEAR WOMEN WHOM I HAVE JUST OFFENDED BY THE USE OF HYSTERIA, WOMAN, AND FAIRER SEX IN LESS THAN 2 LINES, I'M SORRY. I REALLY AM. I WAS RAISED BY WOMEN WHO ARE STRONG, POWERFUL, SMART, AND SILENT. AND SOMETIMES I AM SO ANNOYED BY WOMEN WHO ARE NOT. IT'S JUST A NOTE, AND IT IS JUST WHAT I THINK SOMETIMES. PLEASE KNOW I VALUE YOU AS STRONG, POWERFUL WOMEN WHO HAVE AN OPINION ABOUT MY CHOICE OF WORDS. THANK YOU FOR READING ME ANYWAY.

TO THE WOMAN IN THE BRIGHT PINK GOLF OUTFIT

TO THE WOMAN IN THE BRIGHT PINK GOLF OUTFIT WHO WASHED HER FEET IN THE SINK OF THE RESORT   I'VE GOT NOTHING.

TO PEOPLE WHO MOVE TABLES

TO PEOPLE WHO MOVE TABLES TOGETHER IN RESTAURANTS, BREAKING UP SECTIONS AT WHIM, MOVING FROM ONE COLLECTION OF TABLES TO ANOTHER--PLEASE JUST STOP. ASK A SERVER FOR HELP, BECAUSE YOU ARE PROBABLY MAKING A MESS OF THEIR FLOORPLAN, THEIR INCOME STREAM, AND THEIR ABILITY TO MANEUVER AROUND YOU.

TO MY 19 YEAR OLD SON

TO MY 19 YEAR OLD SON WHO HAS BECOME HIS OWN MAN: YOU HAVE NO IDEA THE SURGE OF PRIDE I FEEL WHEN I WATCH YOU HOLD A CONVERSATION WITH SOMEONE YOU FIND TO BE YOUR INTELLECTUAL EQUAL. AS YOU'VE GROWN, YOU'VE TAKEN PARTS OF BOTH YOUR FATHER AND ME, AND USED THEM TO CREATE YOUR OWN UNIQUE SENSE OF SELF. I WATCH THE CURVES AND LINES OF YOUR FACE AS YOU SMILE IN HUMOR, OR AS YOU FURROW YOUR BROW IN CONTEMPLATION, OR AS YOU BECOME INTENSE AND FOCUSED. YOUR STRAIGHT NOSE AND THE LINE OF YOUR CHEEKBONE ARE BEAUTIFUL BECAUSE THEY LOOK LIKE MINE, BUT I CAN ONLY CLAIM THE GENETICS--ALL OF THE REST OF IT IS YOURS. MY ADORATION FOR YOU CONTINUES TO GROW AS I HEAR YOU SPEAK YOUR OWN THOUGHTS--ONES I NEVER TAUGHT YOU.

TO THE NEIGHBORS

TO THE NEIGHBORS WHO PUT UP PRIVACY FENCES: THANK YOU. PLEASE SUNBATHE IN THE NUDE IN PEACE.

TO THE GRIZZLED COWBOY

TO THE GRIZZLED COWBOY WITH THE BUSHY BEARD WHO SMELLS OF HORSES AND MANURE: I BET EVERY SINGLE DAY IS A JOY FOR YOU. HORSES HAVE AN EMOTIONAL MATURITY MOST HUMANS CANNOT TOUCH. I BET YOUR EVERY MOMENT, WHETHER SPENT IN SPEECH OR SILENCE IS INCREDIBLE. I IMAGINE THE WARMTH OF THE SUN ON THAT MARE'S BACK, AND HOW IT MUST FEEL TO DRAPE YOURSELF OVER HER AS YOU WORK WITH HER. I KNOW HORSES KNOW MORE THAN WE COULD EVER IMAGINE. YOU ARE A LUCKY MAN.

TO THE YOUNG AND VERY DRUNK INVESTMENT BANKER

TO THE YOUNG AND VERY DRUNK INVESTMENT BANKER WHO TRIED TO SELL A POLICY TO ME AND TONY BECAUSE HE WAS WEARING A ROLEX: YOU FORGOT THREE VERY IMPORTANT THINGS.
1. YOU ARE VERY DRUNK AND WE JUST WALKED IN SOBER.
2. YOU ARE YOUNG AND EXCITED. WE ARE OLD AND JADED--AND UNMARRIED.
3. YOU DON'T EVEN HAVE A BUSINESS CARD IN THE WALLET YOU ARE FUMBLING TO OPEN!

AND ONE THING YOU DON'T KNOW--TONY BOUGHT THAT WATCH OFF A HOOKER IN HONG KONG BECAUSE HE'S A CHEAPSKATE. YOU DO THE MATH.

TO THE VISIONARY

To the visionary who does not feel supported--you probably are not. Because people think in so many different ways, and they may not think about the things you see. Why should they care? They don't care. Your goals mean little to nothing to them. Find, or better, build a team around you that is like-minded and goal oriented so you are all striving for the same ends. Don't settle for less than what you feel is perfect. Don't settle just because they don't see it your way. Keep thinking of solutions. Be positive and weed out the negative so your visions become your reality. You can get what you want.

TO THE STUDENTS

TO THE STUDENTS WHO LOOK BLANKLY AT ME WHEN I ASK THEM IF ANYTHING I'VE SAID IS CAUSING THEM TO HAVE MINOR CONNIPTIONS...DO YOU REACT TO ANYTHING ANYMORE? DO I NEED TO ACTUALLY SING AND DANCE? AND IF I DID, IS THAT WHAT I WANT TO DO TO GET YOUR ATTENTION? WHAT WILL IT TAKE TO INSPIRE YOU TO THINK FOR YOURSELF? I'M TRYING TO FIGURE THAT OUT.

TO THE PEOPLE WHO TAKE EVERYTHING NEGATIVELY

TO THE PEOPLE WHO TAKE EVERYTHING NEGATIVELY AND PERSONALLY...TRUST ME. IT IS NOT PERSONAL. WE ARE ALL DEALING WITH OUR OWN LITTLE DEMONS, WHICH IS WHY THEY HAVE BEEN DEPICTED IN LITERATURE AND ART AS THESE THINGS ON OUR SHOULDER FOR MILLENIA. JUST TAKE A MINUTE AND LOOK AT THE ART OF HIERONYMOUS BOSCH. IT WILL BLOW YOUR MIND. YOUR DEMONS PROBABLY ARE LESS SCARY THAN THE ONES HE PAINTED. I BET.

TO SHARON,

TO SHARON, WHO WAS HITCHHIKING ACROSS THE COUNTRY BECAUSE SHE AND HER HUSBAND COULD NOT AFFORD EVEN A BUS TICKET TO LAS VEGAS, NEVADA, I HAVE NO IDEA WHAT YOU HAVE BEEN THROUGH IN YOUR LIFE, BUT I'M ASSUMING IT HAS NOT BEEN AN EASY ONE. TO EVEN MAKE THE CHOICE TO HITCHHIKE IN TODAY'S CULTURE BLOWS MY MIND. I CANNOT PRESUME TO UNDERSTAND YOUR LIFE OR YOUR DECISIONS. I CANNOT PRESUME TO EVEN FATHOM WHAT IT MUST TAKE TO GET BY SOMETIMES. BUT I KNOW THAT IF YOU WERE MY SISTER, OR MY DAUGHTER, OR MY MOTHER, OR MY AUNT, I WOULD NEVER HAVE LET YOU DO THIS ON YOUR OWN WITHOUT A SAFETY NET. I HOPE THINGS WORK OUT FOR YOU.

DEAR READER,

    DEAR READER, FORGIVE ME FOR BREAKING MY STRIDE TO INCLUDE THIS, BUT I'M STRUGGLING WITH MY NEXT NOTE. AS I WAS DROPPING SHARON OFF AT THE BUS DEPOT, I PARKED MY CAR IN A PUBLIC LOT AND SAW A MAN SHADOW BOXING AND LEAPING OFF THE GROUND IN AN APPARENT ATTEMPT TO EITHER 1.) BE A SUPER HERO OR 2.) FIGHT OFF SOMETHING. I SHOOK MY HEAD, BECAUSE WHAT ELSE COULD I DO? HE IS OBVIOUSLY TRIPPING ON SOMETHING, AND I HOPE THAT HELP FINDS HIM. PERHAPS I SHOULD HAVE DONE MORE, BUT I ASK AGAIN, WHAT COULD I DO? I KNOW NOTHING ABOUT ANYTHING THAT PERTAINS TO WHAT I WAS WITNESSING. DRUGS SUCK. WHAT THEY DO TO FAMILIES AND PEOPLE AND IDEALS JUST SUCKS.

TO THE TYPE A LEADER

TO THE TYPE A LEADER WHO IS ALSO IMPATIENT, SLOW IT DOWN, SISTER. IT WILL COME TOGETHER, JUST LIKE A WEDDING. NOBODY KNOWS WHAT YOU HAVE IN MIND, SO IF YOU DO HALF OF WHAT YOU INTEND, THEY WILL BE SURPRISED, ASTONISHED, APPRECIATIVE AND GRATIFIED.

DEAR READER,

 DEAR READER, I'VE BEEN THINKING ABOUT LOVE. IS IT CHEMICAL? IS IT PHYSICAL (AND THEREFORE, CHEMICAL)? IS IT SIMPLY A CHOICE WE MAKE? I SEE SO MANY COUPLES OF DIFFERENT SIZES, SHAPES, BACKGROUNDS, SEXES, AGES, ...AND A LOT OF THEM LAST FOR A LOT OF YEARS. HOW? I'VE BEEN VERY SUCCESSFUL IN LIFE AND IN MY CAREER...BUT LOVE? NOT SO MUCH. MY BEST FRIEND IS CURRENTLY IN HER THIRD MARRIAGE AND SHE TELLS ME, "IF THIS ONE DOESN'T WORK...I'M CONVINCED IT NEVER WILL."
AT ANY RATE--LOVE IS HARD. I WAS ONLY MARRIED ONCE, BUT I'VE HAD MY SHARE OF BOYFRIENDS WHO HAVE MADE ME CRAVE MORE, BETTER LOVE, AND I HAVE HAD BOYFRIENDS WHO HAVE CURED ME OF MY LOVE.

TO EX-BOYFRIENDS

TO EX-BOYFRIENDS WHO FIND IT NECESSARY TO "CHECK IN ON ME" DAYS, WEEKS, MONTHS, OR EVEN YEARS LATER. WHY? WHAT DO YOU HOPE TO ACCOMPLISH? YOU LEFT ONCE, YOU'LL LEAVE AGAIN. I HAVEN'T CHANGED...MUCH. I MEAN, NOW I KNOW THAT YOU WERE NOT THE MAN I THOUGHT YOU WERE, OR THAT I'M NOT THE WOMAN YOU THOUGHT I WAS. AND THAT'S PERFECTLY FINE...NOW. I MAY BE DIFFERENT, BUT I'M STILL THAT BEAUTIFUL, TALENTED, SPIRITED WOMAN I WAS WHEN YOU KNEW ME LAST, AND WHEN YOU HELD ME IN YOUR HANDS AND IN YOUR HEART. NOTHING IN THAT REGARD HAS CHANGED. BUT I KNOW ME BETTER NOW. SO YOU SHOULD REALLY STOP "CHECKING IN ON ME." I'M GOOD. BUT THANKS FOR ASKING.

TO EX-GIRLFRIENDS

TO EX-GIRLFRIENDS OF MEN WHO KEEP "CHECKING IN ON YOU." DON'T RECYCLE. I MEAN, SURE. RECYCLE GLASS, PAPER, ALUMINUM, THAT SORT OF THING. BUT MEN? NOPE. DON'T DO IT. THEY DON'T DESERVE YOU ANY LONGER. THEY LEFT ONCE, DIDN'T THEY? SO MOVE ON, NOW, SISTER. LEAVE HIM FOR SOMEONE ELSE TO WORK ON. YOU ARE WORTH MORE.

TO THE WOMEN WHO RECYCLE

TO THE WOMEN WHO RECYCLE BOYFRIENDS ANYWAY...I GET IT. THERE IS FAMILIARITY, RIGHT? HAVING HISTORY SOMETIMES IS MORE COMFORTABLE THAN THE ABYSS OF LONELINESS. EVEN IF THE HISTORY IS LESS THAN BEAUTIFUL. ROSE COLORED GLASSES AND ALL

TO EMERGENCY ROOM NURSES--

TO EMERGENCY ROOM NURSES--THANK YOU. WHERE WOULD I BE WITHOUT YOU? I MEAN, ACTUALLY, I MIGHT BE DEAD A TIME OR TWO, SO THANK YOU FOR NOT LETTING THAT HAPPEN. THANK YOU ESPECIALLY TO THOSE OF YOU WHO HAVE BEEN COMPASSIONATE AND CONSIDERATE ENOUGH TO HOLD MY HAND WHEN I'M TERRIFIED, ANGRY, HURT, BLEEDING, DESTROYED, AND BROKEN. THANK YOU FOR GIVING ME SOME HUMANITY WHEN EVERYTHING IS BRIGHT LIGHTS AND PAIN AND AGONY.

TO DOCTORS AND NURSES

TO DOCTORS AND NURSES WHO TREAT BREAST CANCER IN ALL OF ITS NEFARIOUS FORMS. THANK YOU, FROM THE BOTTOM OF THE HEART, FOR SAVING TWO OF THE WOMEN WHO MEAN THE MOST TO ME IN MY LIFE. I DON'T SHOW THESE TWO WOMEN ENOUGH HOW IMPORTANT THEY ARE TO ME, BUT KNOWING THAT YOU ARE WORKING TO KEEP THEM HEALTHY AND STRONG SO THEY CAN BE THE BEAUTIFUL, PRODUCTIVE MEMBERS OF SOCIETY THAT THEY ARE, MEANS THE WORLD TO ME. KEEP UP THE GOOD WORK. KEEP UP THE GOOD FAITH.

TO TESTOSTERONE GUY IN THE GYM:

TO TESTOSTERONE GUY IN THE GYM: PLEASE STOP CLANGING THE WEIGHTS. IT'S DISTRACTING WHEN YOU POUND OUT A SET, MOVE TO THE NEXT MACHINE WITH YOUR GRUNTS AND FLEXES AND ANGRY GLARE, THEN DO IT AGAIN ON THE NEXT MACHINE. AND YOU DO THIS IN SUPER AND GIANT SETS, MAKING IT REALLY HARD FOR ANYONE TO DO ANYTHING AROUND YOU. MAYBE THAT'S WHY YOU COME EARLY IN THE MORNING, AND I THINK YOU'RE PROBABLY REALLY INTERESTING, BUT RIGHT NOW, YOU ARE FRIGHTENING AND LOUD.

TO THE PEOPLE WHO THINK THAT NOBODY GETS YOU

TO THE PEOPLE WHO THINK THAT NOBODY GETS YOU...I GET IT, AT THE VERY LEAST. I MIGHT NOT GET YOU, BUT I UNDERSTAND THE FEELING OF FRUSTRATION, HOPELESSNESS, IRRITATION...THE LACK OF WORDS TO EXPLAIN AND ARTICULATE HOW EXACTLY YOU DO FEEL RIGHT AT THIS MOMENT. I GET THAT. SOMETIMES I TRY, AND SOMETIMES I DON'T, BUT SOMETIMES WHEN I TRY, IT TURNS INTO A BEAUTIFUL BRAINSTORM--LIKE WRITING THE NOTES TO PEOPLE THAT I DON'T TAKE THE MOMENT TO SAY WHEN I SHOULD SAY THEM. HANG IN THERE, TOOTS. SOMEONE, AT SOME POINT, WILL EVENTUALLY "GET YOU." SOMEONE, AT SOME POINT, WILL EVENTUALLY GET ME TOO.

TO THE YOUNG FATHER

TO THE YOUNG FATHER WHO WAS SO ENGROSSED IN HIS PHONE THAT HE DID NOT REALIZE HIS DAUGHTER AND HIS OWN FATHER WERE PLAYING WITH THE PAPER TOWELS IN THE CART. YOU TOOK THEM AWAY FROM HER AND MADE HER CRY, THEN TURNED BACK TO YOUR PHONE. YOUR FATHER, IN HIS WILLINGNESS TO LET YOU BE HER FATHER, DIDN'T SAY A WORD. BUT WHAT YOU DID, WITHOUT EVEN REALIZING IT, WAS DESTROY A MOMENT OF PEACE AND SERENITY AND EVEN, I MIGHT SAY, A LEARNING EXPERIENCE FOR YOUR DAUGHTER. AND A MEMORY FOR YOUR FATHER. BECAUSE THAT PHONE HAD YOUR ATTENTION, INSTEAD OF THE PEOPLE WHO SHOULD HAVE MEANT THE MOST TO YOU. WE SPEND SO MUCH TIME IN NEGLECT OF THE THINGS THAT MATTER.

TO THE PERSON WHO FIRST

TO THE PERSON WHO FIRST PUT CARAMEL ON APPLES. WHAT WERE YOU THINKING? AND WERE YOU NOMINATED FOR SAINTHOOD?

TO THE YOUNG WOMEN

TO THE YOUNG WOMEN, AND EVEN THE YOUNG MEN WHO SPEAK IN "VOCAL FRY TONES," STOP IT. USE YOUR DIAPHRAGM AND PROJECT YOUR VOICE. GIVE YOUR WORDS THE POWER THEY DESERVE. YOU KNOW WHAT I'M TALKING ABOUT. IT'S THAT GRAINY, ALMOST WHINY TONE THAT GIVES YOU AN AFFECT OF LAZINESS OR DISREGARD. CUT IT OUT. GIVE WHAT YOU ARE SAYING POWER. GIVE IT THE PURPOSE IT DESERVES.

TO PAINTERS WHO TRULY CAN PAINT,

TO PAINTERS WHO TRULY CAN PAINT, HOLY COW. PAINT LIKE THE WIND, BULLSEYE. IF I COULD PAINT A SUNSET LIKE SOME OF YOU CAN, I DON'T KNOW IF I WOULD EVER BE SATISFIED DOING ANYTHING ELSE. NATURE IS A WONDER, AND YOU HAVE THE EYE AND THE ABILITY TO RECREATE THAT. IT JUST BLOWS MY MIND. PLEASE, PAINT MORE.

TO THE FRIENDS WHO TEXT ME OUT OF THE BLUE

To the friends who text me out of the blue to invite me to "reunion concerts" especially for bands like Foreigner, The Scorpions, Cheap Trick and others, yes, I want to go! I haven't seen you in months, and now I get to see you and them? Uh, duh! Of course I'll be your date!

TO THE INVENTORS OF WHOPPERS

TO THE INVENTORS OF WHOPPERS...YUM.

TO THE MOMS WHO ARE STRUGGLING

TO THE MOMS WHO ARE STRUGGLING TO KEEP THEIR COOL, AND THE MOMS WHO ARE STRUGGLING TO KEEP THEIR CHILDREN AFLOAT, AND TO THE MOMS WHO ARE STRUGGLING IN GENERAL...OH, MOMS. YOU'VE GOT THIS, SISTERS. YOU WERE CREATED TO GIVE LIFE, YOU WERE CREATED TO NURTURE LIFE, AND YOU WERE CREATED TO SURVIVE THIS LIFE. YOU CAN LOOK AT EACH MOMENT UNIQUELY, AND YOU CAN SURVIVE IT, AND YOU CAN THRIVE IN IT. KEEP TRUDGING FORWARD. KEEP PUTTING THAT NEXT FOOT FORWARD, WHETHER IT IS YOUR BEST FOOT OR NOT. KEEP DOING IT. KEEP REMEMBERING THAT YOU HAVE PURPOSE. YOU HAVE VALUE, AND YOU ARE DEFINITELY LOVED.

TO THE LONELY PERSON

TO THE LONELY PERSON WHO HAS ASKED FRIENDS TO MEET AND BEEN REJECTED OVER AND OVER, DON'T LET IT GET YOU DOWN. PICK UP A BOOK AND LET YOURSELF BE YOUR OWN COMPANY. I AM OFTEN MY OWN COMPANY, AND THE BEST PART ABOUT THAT? I'M ALWAYS RIGHT. NOBODY ARGUES WITH ME. NOBODY AGREES WITH ME, EITHER. I MEAN, I AGREE WITH MYSELF, AND THAT'S ALL GOOD, I'M MY BEST COUNSEL, RIGHT? BUT SERIOUSLY, YOU ARE ENOUGH. ENJOY THE PEACE AND QUIET AND THE SERENITY THAT YOU CREATE.

DEAR MAN IN THE GROCERY STORE

DEAR MAN IN THE GROCERY STORE WHO LOOKED AT ME UNTIL YOU REALIZED I WAS LOOKING BACK AT YOU: YOU DIDN'T HAVE TO WAIT FOR ME TO SMILE AT YOU. IF YOU WERE TRYING TO DECIDE WHETHER YOU HAD SEEN ME BEFORE, OR IF YOU KNEW ME FROM SOMEWHERE, THE ANSWER IS, MAYBE. WE DO LIVE IN A SMALL TOWN. AND REALLY, I MEAN, YOUR SMILE WAS BEAUTIFUL. YOU SHOULD SHARE IT MORE OFTEN. I DON'T KNOW THE REASON WHY MEN DO NOT ENGAGE A WOMAN WHEN HE FINDS HER ATTRACTIVE. IT ABSOLUTELY COULD HAVE TO DO WITH THE WAY WE HAVE BEEN SOCIALIZED. OFTEN, HOWEVER, I WOULD WELCOME THE OPPORTUNITY TO HAVE A QUICK CONVERSATION AFTER HAVING BEEN SMILED AT. WHO KNOWS. WE MIGHT HAVE BEEN MADE FOR ONE ANOTHER.

TO THE SURVIVORS:

TO THE SURVIVORS: I AGREE. CANCER SUCKS. I HOPE YOU EXPERIENCE CONTINUAL HEALTH, AND I HOPE THAT IT NEVER DARKENS YOUR DOOR AGAIN. TO MY MOTHER, WHO WATCHED MY FATHER DIE OF CANCER, I AM GLAD HE HAD YOU TO LOVE HIM STILL. TO MY SIBLINGS, WHO WATCHED MY FATHER DIE, I WISH WE HAD NEVER GIVEN HIM THE MEDICINE THAT ACTUALLY KILLED HIM. I MISS HIM TOO. TO MY SON, WHO WANTED TO KNOW HIS GRANDFATHER BETTER, HE WAS A WONDERFUL, GRAINY, GRUMPY, FUNNY OLD MAN WHO ONCE WAS YOUNG AND FULL OF ADVENTURE. TO HILARY, WHO HAD BREAST CANCER AND LIVES IN FEAR OF IT ALWAYS, YOU'RE AMAZING. TO KRISTY, WHO HAS HAD IT TWICE, I HOPE CANCER NEVER FINDS YOU AGAIN. TO SUSIE, WHO WORRIES THAT HER CANCER WILL KEEP HER FROM CELEBRATING CHRISTMAS WITH HER KIDS, KEEP FIGHTING. FOR ANYONE ELSE WHO ACHES FROM THIS DISEASE, HOLD ON TO THE GOOD THINGS. AND THAT IS WHAT I SAY TO ANY SURVIVOR.

TO THE STRONG SILENT TYPE,

TO THE STRONG SILENT TYPE, I WISH I COULD BE MORE LIKE YOU. I HAVE MUCH TO SAY, AND I AM OFTEN THOUGHTFUL, BUT I WISH I HAD LESS TO SAY AND MORE TO OBSERVE. THAT'S NOT TO SAY THAT ALL OF YOU QUIET TYPES ARE ACTUALLY SPENDING TIME OBSERVING. YOU KNOW SOME OF YOU ARE TOTALLY DAYDREAMING UP IN THERE.

TO THE NEIGHBORS WHO JUST MOVED OUT...

TO THE NEIGHBORS WHO JUST MOVED OUT...SIGH. WHY IS YOUR FURNITURE LEFT ON THE FRONT PORCH? I REALLY LIKE THAT SET OF KITCHEN CHAIRS. WILL YOU BE PICKING THOSE UP ANY TIME SOON? YES, I'M PROBABLY A HOARDER. NO, IT'S NOT A PROBLEM.

TO THE HEN-PECKED HUSBAND

TO THE HEN-PECKED HUSBAND WHO HAS SET UP A SPACE TO SLEEP WHEN HE AND HIS WIFE FIGHT...YOU COULD TELL YOUR SISTER, YOU KNOW. SHE'D SET YOU UP WITH A HOT DISH OF SPAGHETTI, A COLD GLASS OF SOMETHING TO DRINK, AND YOU WOULDN'T HAVE TO TELL HER ANYTHING ABOUT ANYTHING IF YOU DIDN'T WANT TO. ESPECIALLY BECAUSE SHE ISN'T EVEN SUPPOSED TO KNOW THAT YOU HAVE SET THIS SPACE UP IN THE EVENT THAT YOU FIGHT WITH YOUR WIFE. BECAUSE GOOD HUSBANDS DON'T AIR DIRTY LAUNDRY. AND IF YOUR WIFE DOESN'T SEE THAT IN YOU, AND ONLY SEES YOUR FLAWS, THEN KNOW THAT SHE'S A FOOL.

TO THE FELLA IN SPROUTS

   TO THE FELLA IN SPROUTS WHO IS NOT WEARING ANY SHOES. YOU ARE SUPER TALL AND HAVE REALLY LONG HAIR, AND I'M NOT JUDGING YOU, BUT I KIND OF AM. YOU CAN'T WALK IN THE GROCERY STORE WITHOUT SHOES. IT'S REALLY NOT VERY HYGIENIC. I MEAN...I'VE BEEN IN THAT STORE AND HAVE SEEN WHAT GETS SPILLED BY OTHER PATRONS. I'VE BEEN THERE WITH CHILDREN AND I KNOW THAT CHILDREN DROP FOOD AND THEN PICK IT UP. WHERE HAVE YOUR FEET BEEN? WHERE HAS THAT CHILD BEEN? I GET IT THAT YOUR SKIN IS KIND OF LIKE A GIANT PIECE OF SARAN WRAP, AND IT IS DESIGNED TO PROTECT YOU FROM GERMS, BUT THERE ARE LIMITS. AND THAT IS JUST GROSS.

TO THE TALL MOUNTAIN OF A MAN

TO THE TALL MOUNTAIN OF A MAN IN THE PINK SOFTBALL JERSEY ON THE LAS VEGAS STRIP: WOW. ON FIRST GLANCE, I THOUGHT IT HUMOROUS THAT YOU WORE YOUR PINK JERSEY ADVERTISING THAT YOU WERE A MEMBER OF A TEAM HERE FOR THE TOURNAMENT, BUT THEN I REALIZED I MOSTLY NOTICED YOU BECAUSE YOU TOWER OVER ALL OF THE REST OF US. YOU ARE AT LEAST 6'3", MAYBE 6'4", AND I"M A MERE 5'3", EVEN THOUGH I ALWAYS THINK I'M MUCH BIGGER. YOU DWARF ME, AND REALLY, EVERY SINGLE OTHER PERSON IN THIS PLACE. IT'S NICE TO MEET YOU, TALL GUY. I BET A LOT OF PEOPLE ASK YOU IF YOU PLAY BASKETBALL. EVERY TALL GUY HAS TO HAVE PLAYED BASKETBALL, RIGHT?

TO THE MEN AND WOMEN WHO HAVE THIS PATTERN

TO THE MEN AND WOMEN WHO HAVE THIS PATTERN OF "GHOSTING" ONE ANOTHER, I JUST HAVE ONE QUESTION: WHY? HARD CONVERSATIONS ARE JUST THAT--HARD. BUT NOT IMPOSSIBLE. DO YOU RESPECT YOURSELF? DID YOU RESPECT THE OTHER AT ONE POINT? DON'T YOU BOTH OWE IT TO YOURSELVES TO HAVE THOSE DIFFICULT, OR MAYBE, NOT EVEN SO DIFFICULT CONVERSATIONS, AND, INSTEAD, JUST GET SOME CLARITY AND PEACE? I GUESS I HAD MORE THAN 1 QUESTION. IT JUST MATTERS. WE LIVE IN A CULTURE OF DISRESPECT. WE LIVE IN AN ERA OF VICTIMIZING, SHAMING, AND WITCH HUNTING. LET'S BE REAL, PEOPLE, AND TAKE CARE OF EACH OTHERS' HEARTS. IT JUST DOESN'T COST ANYTHING.

TO THE HEAVYSET WOMAN WHO HAS DUCT-TAPED HER BREASTS,

TO THE HEAVYSET WOMAN WHO HAS DUCT-TAPED HER BREASTS, PUT ON A PAIR OF BOY SHORTS AND A TUTU TO STAND IN THE CHILLY AIR OF THE LAS VEGAS STRIP EVENING TO MAKE SOME CASH...DO YOU REALLY MAKE ENOUGH MONEY TO JUSTIFY SELLING YOUR BODY LIKE THIS?

TO THE MAN WHO BUSTED ME

TO THE MAN WHO BUSTED ME TAKING PICTURES OF HIM ON THE STREET: I WAS INSPIRED! I KNOW, I KNOW, I'M A *STALKER* OBSERVER. I'M SORRY! BUT THANKS FOR NOT STEALING MY PHONE AND DELETING YOUR IMAGE!

TO MY SON:

TO MY SON: I DON'T HAVE ALL THE ANSWERS. I'M SORRY.

TO WIELAND,

TO WIELAND, WHO GOES TO THE RESORT ONCE A MONTH, DRINKS ONE DRAFT BEER AND READS WHILE HE WAITS FOR HIS WIFE TO GET HER HAIR DONE...YOU ARE THE SWEETEST OLD AUSTRIAN I'VE EVER MET. YOUR MIND IS SHARP AND YOUR WIT SHARPER, THOUGH YOUR WORDS COME SLOWLY. I LOOK FORWARD TO OUR VISITS OVER YOUR BEER AND YOUR BOOK. WHEN YOU DON'T SHOW FOR LONG PERIODS OF TIME, I WORRY ABOUT YOU, BECAUSE I THINK YOU MUST BE CLOSE TO 100. YOU ARE A SPARK IN THE DAY.

TO THE WOMAN WHO WEARS TOO MUCH MAKEUP

TO THE WOMAN WHO WEARS TOO MUCH MAKEUP AND HAS A VERY UNFORTUNATE SWEATER ON, WHAT GIVES YOU THE RIGHT TO BE SO MEAN TO YOUR SERVER? SHE DIDN'T ASK WHAT TYPE OF CHARDONNAY YOU WANTED BECAUSE THERE IS ONLY ONE CHARDONNAY ON THE MENU. YOU DON'T HAVE TO BE RUDE AND MAKE SURE SHE HEARS YOU. YOU CAN, INSTEAD, SIT BACK A SEC AND THINK ABOUT IT. AND IF YOU MUST COMMENT, WHICH I KNOW YOU MUST, BE QUIETER ABOUT IT!

TO THE HOMELESS MAN

To the homeless man who spent his afternoon cleaning up the trash and debris left behind by others, rather than sitting morosely with your cardboard...I wish I had more money to give you. I appreciate you so much. I don't know the story that found you where you are now, but I know that you know where you want to be, and you know how you are getting there.

TO THE FATHER OF THE FIVE YEAR OLD

TO THE FATHER OF THE FIVE YEAR OLD WHO IS WATCHING YOUR PHONE WHILE YOU SIT NEXT TO HIM, POLISHING OFF YOUR DINNER. HEADPHONES...OR CONVERSATION. DO YOU REALLY WANT TO RAISE HIM THE EASY WAY, WITH A TV IN FRONT OF HIM? YOU ARE MISSING A BEAUTIFUL OPPORTUNITY TO INSTRUCT AND GUIDE HIM, AND I CAN ONLY ASSUME IT IS BECAUSE YOU ARE TIRED OF TALKING TO A LITTLE KID ABOUT LITTLE KID THINGS. SO SPEAK TO HIM ABOUT HOW HE CAN BE A BETTER PERSON, OR LET HIM TEACH YOU TO BE A BETTER PERSON. THE PHONE AND YOUTUBE IS JUST TOO EASY.

TO THE TEENAGED GIRL

TO THE TEENAGED GIRL WHO TRIED TO RACE TRAFFIC AND CATCH HER MUCH FASTER FRIENDS WHO HAD ALREADY BEGUN TO CROSS THE ROAD-- SISTER. YOU DROPPED YOUR PHONE IN THE MIDDLE OF THE 5 LANED ROAD, AND THEN, EVEN THOUGH WE WERE BARRELING DOWN ON YOU, YOU TURNED TO GO BACK FOR IT! NO THING IS WORTH YOUR LIFE, ESPECIALLY NOT YOUR PHONE. I AM SO GRATEFUL THAT IT WAS AIDAN DRIVING, AND THE HE HAS THE MIND OF A STEEL TRAP, HE ASSESSED THE SITUATION, AND HAD YOU PEGGED. HE SAVED YOUR LIFE.

TO THE WOMAN WHO

To the woman who not only pulled the shopping cart up on the median, but also drove it over three feet of large grade river rock so you could avoid banging your car door on it...why didn't you just walk it across the aisle and put it back in the shopping cart corral? I mean, you worked harder in the end, to put it on the median than the energy it would have taken to walk it 12 feet. You are a curious sort.

DEAR SWEET STUDENT OF MINE

DEAR SWEET STUDENT OF MINE WHO JUST LOST HER MOTHER...THERE ARE NO WORDS THAT I CAN SAY TO YOU TO MAKE YOU FEEL BETTER. IT WOULDN'T MATTER IF YOU WERE 17, 27, 47 OR ANY OTHER AGE. THE ONLY THING I KNOW FOR CERTAIN IS THE THING SOMEONE TOLD ME WHEN I LOST MY FATHER, AND THAT IS THAT IT WILL NEVER REALLY GET "BETTER." IT WILL ONLY GET "DIFFERENT." YOUR HEART IS STRONGER THAN YOU REALIZE.

TO THE TWO PEOPLE WHO EFFECTIVELY STEMMED

TO THE TWO PEOPLE WHO EFFECTIVELY STEMMED THE FLOW OF TRAFFIC IN THE GROCERY STORE BY STOPPING YOUR CARTS MOSTLY NEXT TO EACH OTHER, EVEN THOUGH YOU HAD "PASSED" ONE ANOTHER. YOU ALSO TOOK A FULL FOOT ON EITHER SIDE OF YOUR CART SO THAT YOU COULD LOOK AT THE CANNED GOODS. I'M STUCK HERE (ON MY PHONE...HEHEHEH) WHILE I TRY TO PAY ATTENTION TO MY SISTER, AND ALSO NAVIGATE YOUR TRAFFIC JAM. I'M NOT BEING SUCCESSFUL. MY SISTER HAS NOW PUT ME ON HOLD, SO, OH! WAIT! THANK YOU, OLD MAN! YOU MOVED YOUR CART. I'M OUT OF HERE.

TO YOUNG PARENTS WHO ARE THINKING

TO YOUNG PARENTS WHO ARE THINKING ABOUT THEIR YOUNG CHILDREN: PLEASE, PLEASE, PLEASE...READ TO YOUR KIDS. READ THEM THINGS YOU LIKE, READ THEM THINGS THEY LIKE, READ ALOUD ALL THE TIME. MY BEST SUGGESTION? READ FABLES, FAIRY TALES AND RHYMES TO THEM. INTRODUCE THEM TO THINGS THAT HAVE LESSONS AND RHYTHMS AND THAT INTRIGUE THEM AND MAKE THEM ASK QUESTIONS. I PROMISE-- THOSE FEW MINUTES BEFORE BED ARE THE MOST REWARDING OF YOUR DAY, AND OF THEIR LIVES.

TO THE KID WITH THE RED HAIR

TO THE KID WITH THE RED HAIR AND THE WHITE FRAMED EYEGLASSES, YOU DISARMED ME. I WAS COLD AND GRUMPY AND TIRED AND WANTED TO GET HOME AND YOU WERE TOO YOUNG TO BE CERTIFIED TO SERVE ALCOHOL TO THE LADY IN LINE BEFORE ME. YOUR VOICE GRATED ON ME, SO I WAS IRRITATED TO BE DISARMED. YOU TOLD ME I HAD PRETTY EYES, AND THAT DISTRACTED ME FROM MY IRRITATION. THANK YOU FOR BEING BETTER THAN ME. YOU REMINDED ME I COULD BE BETTER.

TO THE PEOPLE WHO LEAVE TRASH

TO THE PEOPLE WHO LEAVE TRASH IN THE WILD, I JUST WANT TO ASK YOU WHY YOU DO THAT. CARELESSNESS? NEGLIGENCE? THE THOUGHT THAT SOMEONE ELSE WILL CLEAN UP AFTER YOU? IT JUST DOESN'T MAKE SENSE TO THROW A GLASS BOTTLE INTO A RIVER WHERE PEOPLE SWIM, OR TO TOSS PLASTIC ON THE SAND DUNES, OR TO LEAVE YOUR DIRTY DIAPERS ON THE RIVERBANK. TO ME, NATURE IS BEAUTIFUL BECAUSE IT IS NATURE. I GO TO IT TO ESCAPE HUMANS, AS I BET YOU DID TOO. WHY DO YOU LEAVE YOUR MARK NO MATTER WHERE YOU GO? PACK IT IN, PACK IT OUT. IT IS PROBABLY EASIER TO PACK IT OUT, IN FACT, THAN IT WAS TO PACK IT IN.

TO THE MAN WHO WATCHES

TO THE MAN WHO WATCHES IN THE GYM, WEIRD. BUT THEN AGAIN, I'VE LEARNED THAT I AM A STARER IN BETWEEN SETS, SO IS IT SO MUCH WEIRDER FOR A MAN TO STARE THAN FOR A WOMAN? I AM JUST AS WEIRD, I THINK. I DON'T MEAN TO STARE. I ACTUALLY PROBABLY JUST KICKED MY OWN ASS AND AM STRUGGLING JUST TO BREATHE, AND THAT'S WHY MY EYES ARE GLAZED OVER. PERHAPS THE SAME IS TRUE FOR YOU.

TO THE NEIGHBOR WHO

TO THE NEIGHBOR WHO BRINGS OVER A PLASTIC BAG OF BUD LIGHT, THAT'S KIND OF FUN, BUT I DON'T TRUST YOUR MOTIVATIONS. I HAVE THOUGHT OF WAYS TO DISCOURAGE YOU FROM VISITING, AND IT FASCINATES ME THAT AS A WOMAN I HAVE TO THINK OF THE WAY TO EXPRESS MY OBJECTIONS TO YOU SO I DON'T "HURT YOUR FEELINGS." I HAVE TO WONDER WHAT THOSE MOTIVATIONS ARE, BECAUSE I DON'T TRUST THAT THEY ARE AS INNOCENT AS YOU WOULD TRY TO MAKE ME BELIEVE.

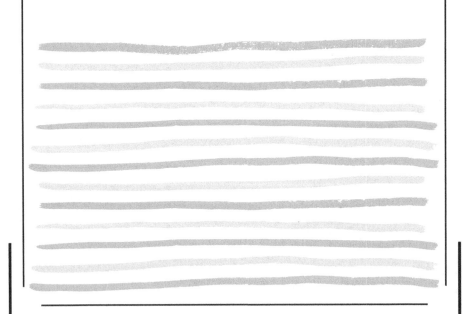

TO THE COP WHO POPPED IN TO CHECK

TO THE COP WHO POPPED IN TO CHECK TO SEE IF I HAD VICIOUS DOGS FIGHTING ON THE PROPERTY...ACTUALLY, THAT WAS COOPER AND DOZER, THE NEIGHBOR DOG. WHEN YOU ARRIVED THEY WERE DANCING AROUND EACH OTHER AND TROTTING THROUGH MY FENCED YARD. SOMEONE CALLED YOU, WORRIED THAT THEY WERE FIGHTING, OR MAYBE THAT I WAS TRAINING FIGHTING DOGS. THAT IS SO FAR FROM THE TRUTH IT IS LAUGHABLE, BUT I'M GLAD YOU STOPPED. YOU COULD SEE FOR YOURSELF THAT THESE DOGS ARE JUST WACKY PUPPIES WHO DON'T EVEN KNOW HOW TO CONTROL THEIR PAWS YET. COOPER DUMPS HIS FOOD AT LEAST ONCE A DAY.

TO MY READERS:

TO MY READERS: I'VE BEEN THINKING ABOUT HOW CRITICAL I AM OF OTHERS IN MANY OF MY COMMENTS HERE. TRUST ME, I'M CRITICAL OF MYSELF TOO. I THINK ABOUT ME AND MY REACTION FIRST, AND THEN I WRITE IT. TO THAT END, I AM GROWING AS A THINKER AND AS A CITIZEN. THE THINGS I THINK I NEED TO SAY SOMETIMES NEED TO NOT BE SAID. I HAD ENVISIONED THIS AS A POSITIVE WAY TO UNBURDEN, BUT AS MY SON SAYS, SOMETIMES, WHEN WE UNBURDEN, IT IS OUT OF SELFISHNESS, RATHER THAN OUT OF GENEROSITY. WHEN I TELL HIM I MISS HIM, I MAKE MYSELF FEEL BETTER, AND HIM, I MAKE FEEL WORSE. IT'S A MEAN CIRCLE OF EMOTIONAL BAGGAGE. THERE ARE MANY MORE NOTES I FEEL I WILL ALWAYS WANT TO WRITE. AND TO THAT END, I BELIEVE THIS BOOK COULD BE NEVERENDING. BUT I MUST FIND AN END TO IT, OR I WILL NEVER BE DONE. WHAT I HAVE LEARNED FROM THIS EXERCISE IS THAT SOME THINGS SHOULD BE SAID, AND SOME THINGS SHOULD BE WRITTEN, AND SOME THINGS SHOULD REMAIN IN THE TEMPORARY ETHER OF NOTHINGNESS AND OF THOUGHT, NOT SPOKEN OR WRITTEN.

I HAD HOPED EVERY COMMENT WOULD BE HAPPY AND POSITIVE. NOT ALL OF THEM ARE. I AM JUDGMENTAL AND CRITICAL. I WRITE THEM SO THE POISON DOESN'T SEEP INTO THE REST OF MY INTERACTIONS WITH OTHERS. PERHAPS I'VE BEEN SUCCESSFUL, PERHAPS THERE IS SO MUCH MORE TO LEARN.

Made in the USA
Middletown, DE
21 July 2024

57814594R00057